Fleas

Written by
Stephen Rickard

Here is a flea.

A flea is a tiny insect. It has six legs.

A flea is this big: •

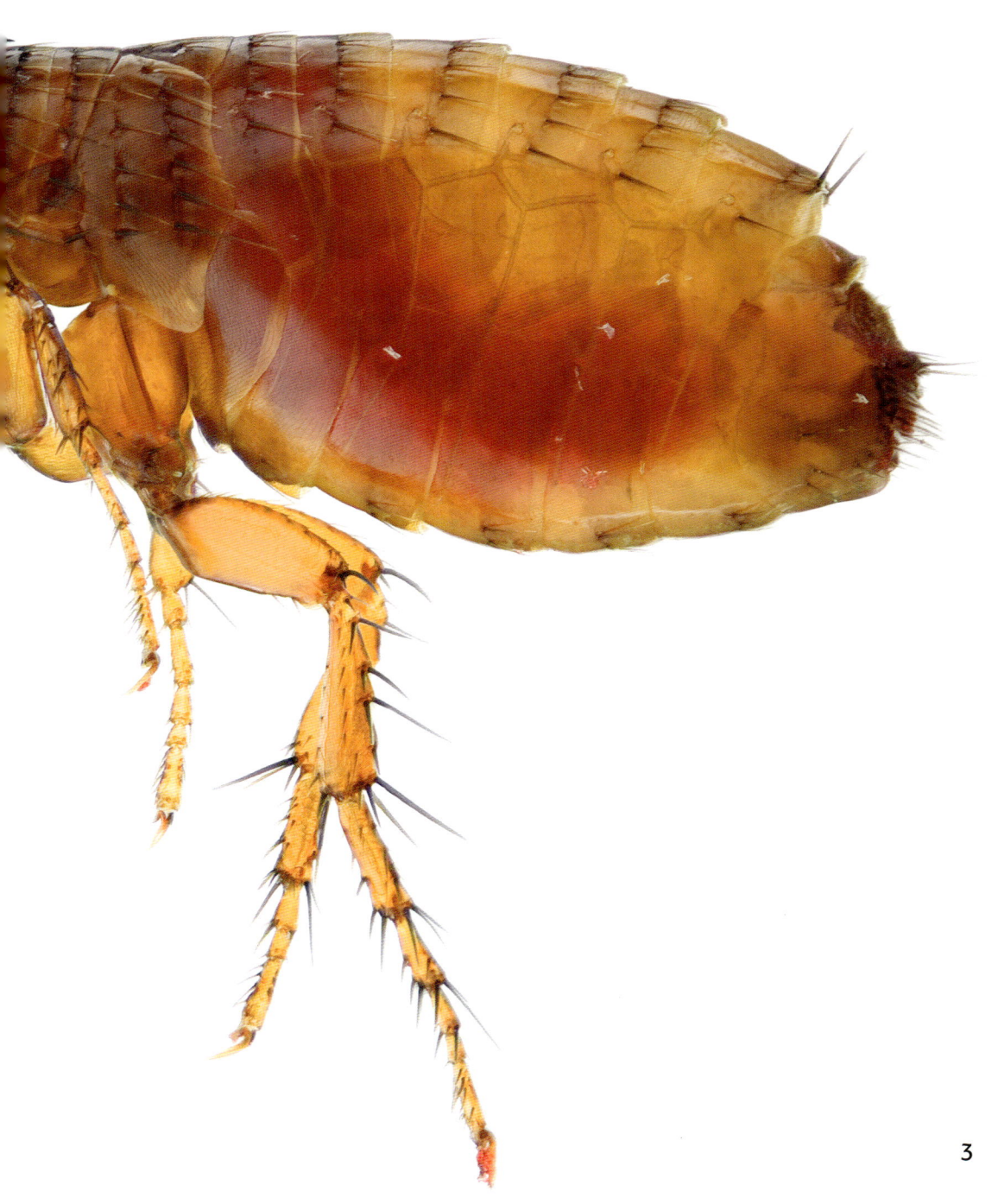

Here is a cat flea.

Cat fleas live on cats and on dogs.

The flea hides in the animal's fur.

It bites the animal and sucks its blood.

Here is a dog flea.

Dog fleas can live on dogs and on cats.

This flea bites humans, too.

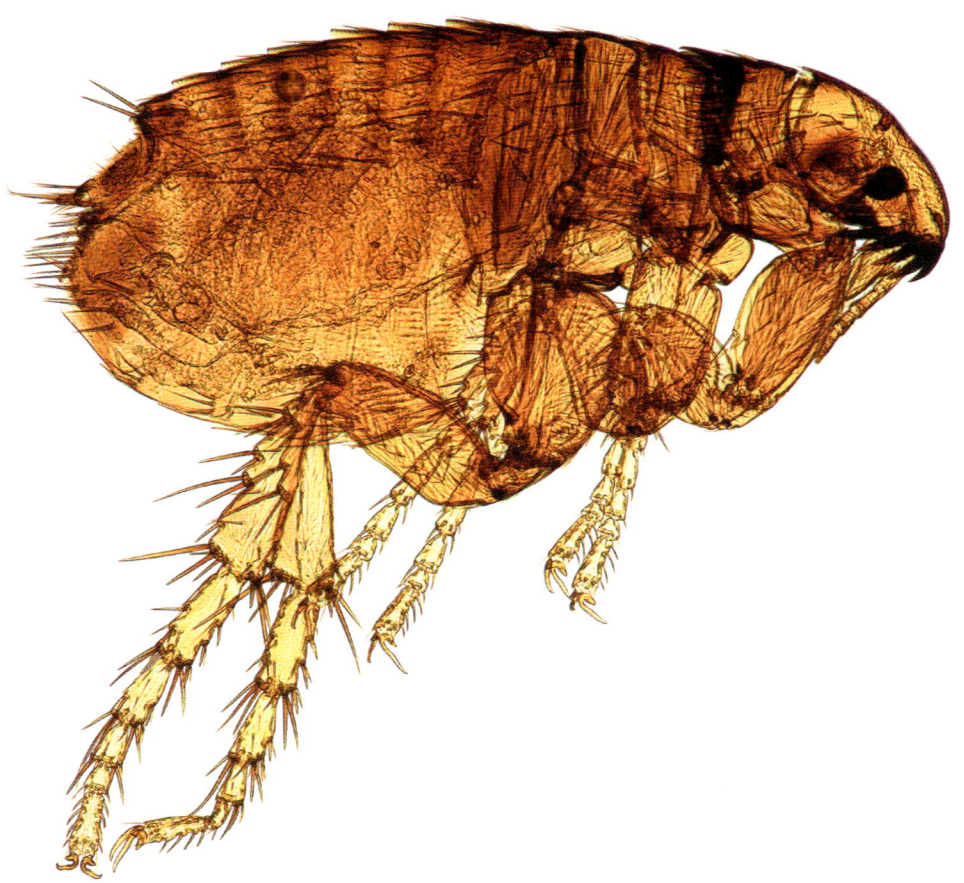

Here is a human flea.

This flea lives on humans and on animals.

This flea lives in human hair.
It bites and sucks our blood.

When you brush your dog,
you may find fleas.

When your cat or dog has fleas, you must get rid of them.

You must visit the vet.

Here is a tick.

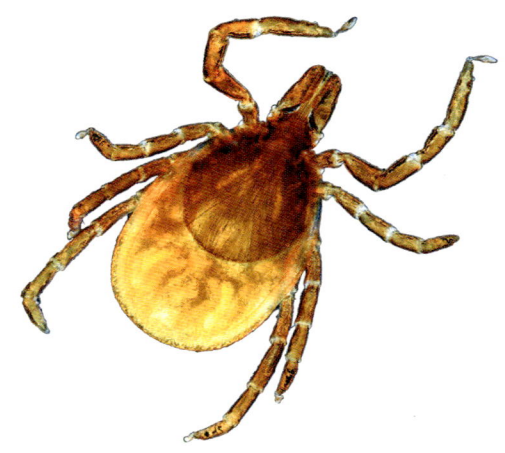

A tick is very small.

A tick is not an insect.
It has eight legs, like a spider.

The tick bites the animal
and sucks its blood, just like a flea.

The tick has sharp teeth.

A tick on human skin

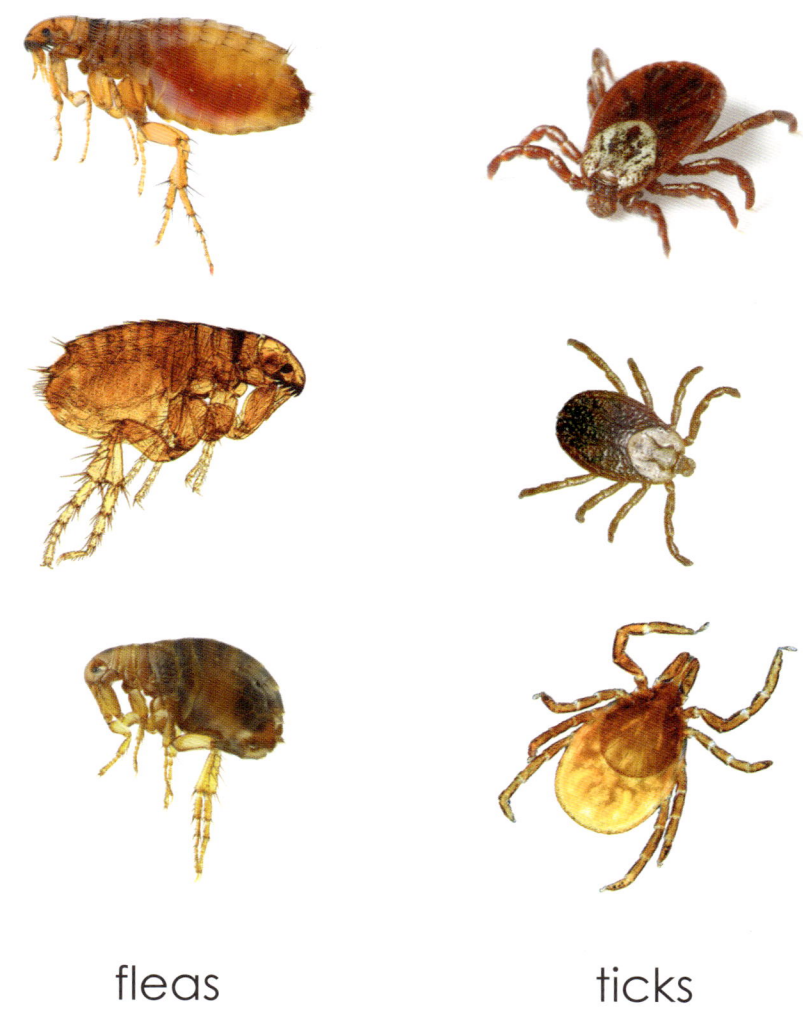

fleas   ticks